I0098774

Momma's Prayer Flags

Momma's Prayer Flags

edited
by
Lorna Crozier

WINTERGREEN
STUDIOS PRESS

Wintergreen Studios Press
Township of South Frontenac
PO Box 75, Yarker, ON, Canada K0K 3N0

Copyright © 2015, with copyright retained by individual authors. All rights reserved under the International and Pan-American Copyright Conventions. No part of this book may be reproduced in any form or by electronic or mechanical means, including information storage and retrieval systems, without permission in writing from the publisher, except by a reviewer, who may quote brief passages in a review. The views expressed in this work are those of the authors and do not necessarily reflect those of the publisher. Wintergreen Studios Press (WSP) gratefully acknowledges the financial support received from Wintergreen Studios.

Book and cover design by Rena Upitis
Edited by Lorna Crozier and Susan Olding
Front artwork: Ink drawing by Melanie Craig-Hansford

Composed in Book Antiqua and Candara, typefaces designed by Monotype Typography and Gary Munch, respectively.

Library and Archives Canada Cataloguing in Publication
Crozier, Lorna.
Momma's Prayer Flags/Lorna Crozier
ISBN: 978-0-9918722-4-4
1.
Poetry – General.
I. Title. Momma's Prayer Flags.
Legal Deposit – Library and Archives Canada

Contents

God Wants to See You

Wintergreen is a place of solace and creativity, meadows and forests and lakes where we as humans, all our senses on high alert, are invited to erase the boundaries between us and other living things. Poetry so happily finds a home here.

This May, twelve of us gathered to roll around in the stink and bones and grit of words. We learned to open ourselves, to be surprised, to see the inner glow of ordinary things. We came to understand the "total depravity / of nettles and nightshade." We read "the literature of snow." We made motel beds with Cordelia and dumplings with Chairman Mao. We picnicked with Mary Oliver, walked with Dr. Spock and went into analysis with Anaïs Nin. We pinned our stories to the line and watched "the bright colours blow dry / In the wind."

And together, writing, and talking and reading every day, we discovered things about others, about ourselves and about the art of poetry. What it's like, for instance, for a woman to "learn too late / she has wasted her life" and that some "secrets should remain just that." We discovered that when you pay close attention to the world, "God wants to see you." We shaped and reshaped our poetry and understood that "force will never bind" the wildness of a poem; "you need to trace their edges with water — that subtle, that slippery element."

What follows are eleven poems that came out of five days together at Wintergreen. The magic and wonder of the place resides in these words.

Lorna Crozier

SUSAN ALEXANDER

Making Beds with Cordelia at the Avalon Motel in Osoyoos, BC, Summer 1973: A Soliloquy

She could sing Desperado just like Linda Ronstadt.
I showed her hospital corners and how to
smooth sheets like my mother taught me.
She didn't have one — a mom.
Thrown out of the house — for nothing
according to her and I believed her,
believed the worst of fathers in general,
temper tantrums, hard hands and drinking.
She wouldn't talk about him, not a thing,
but I remember something about two bitchy sisters —
one with a name like venereal disease
while Cordelia, she walked right out of a magazine
with her long legs and sort of private smile —
smart too though she didn't show off like I did
or mouth off either. I showed her how to
tuck a bedspread under pillows then curve it
snug like a tight t-shirt. She had the knack,
was better than me in more ways than one.
When she wasn't around I pretended —
tried to talk and dress, wear my hair like her,
be patient with my baby brother, be nicer
than I was or am. She lived alone in our shack
out back of the motel beside the slough we called a lake —
saving up for university, she said.

Sometimes after work we'd lie together
under the walnut tree. I'd play with her hair
while she read to me — rich green leaves
breaking the heat of an Okanagan afternoon.
I always thought she'd get discovered
like that dairy queen girl or she'd marry
a millionaire. Strange thing is
I was the one who kind of made it in the end,
the one with the house and European holidays.
But Cordelia, she made headway for awhile,
then somehow it went bad again — a man,
some dark angel, following her.

LAURA APOL

Weeding the Garden with John Calvin †

We agree on the total depravity
of nettles and nightshade,
the unconditional election
of the lavender along the stairs.

But he's inflexible
when I speak of the complexity
of wisteria or Queen Anne's lace,
the original blessing
of raspberry canes.

It's about context and intent,
I explain. *Consider the lily…*

but he has moved on
to limited atonement—
muttering, *Many are called*
but few are chosen as he pulls up
the nasturtium for the fire.

I move fast to rescue
every volunteer sunflower
within reach,
cut the thick stalks.
When he enters the kitchen,
I am arranging them
in a terracotta vase.

He just can't let it go:
Is or is not the sunflower
made in the image of God?
he persists as I work.

I argue that even the sunflower
grows weary under everlasting
scrutiny, its petalled head bowed
with the weight of
irresistible grace.

In the end, we both esteem
the perseverance of its saintly
face, its yellow crown —

the seeds that drop
to once again become a weed,

become a flower.

---

† The five points of Calvin's doctrines are as follows:
Total Depravity, Unconditional Election, Limited Atonement,
Irresistible Grace, Perseverance of the Saints.

MARY LEE BRAGG

The Literature of Snow

Willa Cather's pioneers tell of the Russian wedding
when the groom threw the bride off the sleigh
in a last, doomed, attempt to save himself
from the pursuing wolves.

Steven Heighton's lost Arctic explorers
cut steaks from their dead companions and
make soup from their bones.

Boris Pasternak describes a bullet
slamming into a heart in air so icy
the spray of blood freezes mid-air and
drops roll on the snow like frozen berries.

David Lean filmed Dr. Zhivago in Spain.
The ice-covered dacha where the lovers hide
was really covered in wax. Between takes
the actors stripped and sat in front of fans.

On film, Heighton's explorers could rise
from their soup pots, their bones
reassemble and dance.

Wolves would run backward
drool slurping into their maws
and the bride would jump on the sleigh,
eager for her wedding night.

MAUREEN BAUER-MCGAHEY

Picnic in the Daisy Field With Mary Oliver

"Meet me in the daisy field," the note read.
I grab sunhat, slam screen door, amble through the grass,
climb rail fence to top of the hill.
Wild turkeys stroll the nearby field and woods.
There is Mary — a picnic basket, gingham cloth laid out.
"I have been here all day," she says.

With outstretched palm she says, "Pay attention.
See this grasshopper — this grasshopper I mean — "
"Geez Mary. I get your affinity with bears, geese and swans —
but grasshoppers?"
Ignoring me — "See how this grasshopper has
flung herself out of the grass
and is moving her jaws back and forth instead of up and down."
"Ah Mary? What about the group of wild turkeys
that cavort these fields every morning?"

Mary has one eyeball to the grasshopper now. She says,
"Look how she lifts her pale forearms
and thoroughly washes her face.
Now she snaps her wings open and floats away."

I think to myself, "Thank, God," and try to distract her more.
"Mare — have a sandwich. Here's some watermelon too.
Give yourself a break and put away
that magnifying glass before you start a fire!"
She begins to eat.

Across the field, I notice a turkey fanning his feathers and strutting.
"Why not consider a distraction—a new hobby or a trip?"
"I do know how to pay attention," she says,
"And how to stroll through the fields, which I have doing all day."
"Tell me what else should I have done?"
"I know. But remember the last time you fell into the grass—
You needed physio for months!"

Juices of watermelon drip on her chin and slide down her forearms.
Her jaws move up and down, then back and forth.
I go back to the trip idea.
"How about France, Mare?
There's a Carmelite monastery there.
Remember you confided that you didn't exactly
know what a prayer was.
The monks could fill you in on that.
They pray all the time—24/7.
Oh and they could help you with your other query—
"Who made the world?""

A gunshot sounds.
Our heads swivel.
A huge turkey falls from the rail fence. Dead.
Mary says, "Doesn't everything die at last and too soon?"
I nod in agreement.
Surely, this bird had plans for his one wild and precious life.

SANDRA CAMPBELL

After dinner I tried to do something.

My teacher puts out a call, "Do something with another writer. Or God. Or Buddha."

I have to respond — I am responsible, after all, and sometimes for a moment I think I can do something. Then it passes and I want to move, only I'm not able because I ate too much pasta, drank too much wine.

There are two parts to the call: 'Do something' and 'do it with.' For a moment I wonder who and reach for my books, leaf through my poets. Could be Levertov. She loves what I love — but I hardly know her. Will she say yes? An inner voice interjects, "No way! She's got much bigger fish to fry."

I turn out the lights, stretch out on my bed. There's your breath, I tell myself, and the darkness thrumming with crickets and frogs — companions galore, if you choose — but they're hardly my type.

Sleep comes, but frazzled by Forms. I grasp to write a pantoum, but can only count backwards and as for content, I've not even a first line.

Help! Forget 'doing with.' I need someone to lead. It can't be God or Buddha, I know that much. Too much light — impossible to hide.

At dawn, a weight on my shoulder, a wide-spaded hand that pulls me upwards. The touch tells me it's my dead husband disguised as Wendell Berry and saying his words, "Accept what comes out of silence. Like prayers prayed back to the one who prays."

He leads me outdoors. No silence here. There is birdsong. He leads me into the woods. The hermit thrush sounds around and inside.

God wants to see you.

MELANIE CRAIG-HANSFORD

The Guessing

I tried to paint it once, the brush
felt awkward in my hand
the strokes poisoned our bedroom.

The gesso walls crumbled
under the weight of the impasto,
they would not speak of our afternoons.

Or your silences, when I prayed you
weren't inventing a life without me
by composing brilliant metaphors
for the demise of our relationship.

We met years later in Piazza San Lorenzo;
I wanted to squeeze you out onto the
cobbled stones like crimson paint from a tube.

To get a look inside, to see your
childhood, your adolescent relics,
first communions and lost loves,
your reasons for not following me home.

You turned to stone, in the
piazza, like a masterpiece, hidden;
your secrets shall remain just that. It isn't enough
for me anymore; the guessing.

BARBARA HUNT

To Walk and Talk with Dr. Spock

I always walk since muscle-motion soothes,
so just for kicks I call him
tall and rangy to attend.

Pushing his glasses back good Doctor
pronounces, *You know more than you think you do*
like gospel making my hands itch

to reach out, strangle him. *Fuck off!*
But counting first to 10 then 20, I breathe,
stop short of cramming a sterilized bottle

down his throat. *Where'd you leave the rest
of the Common Sense Book?* I demand
still trying on infanticide or homelessness

my Mummy-brain churns on demand-feedings,
sleeping tummy-or-back and were we wise
to circumcise? *Modern views aren't for everyone,*

his advice ...*50 million copies can't be wrong.*
His brilliant-white coat gives me pause
in helpless, headlong urge to throw

myself from some high bridge. He's gone.
Although still dogged by crying and prepared to go
all 'exorcist' on words like blessing, adorable, cute,

I see his calling was more about comfort than fact.
For who can say, if ever shared, these hard truths
could not put an end to the entire human race.

RUTH MCKINNEY

On Asking My Aunt If She Ever Plays Her Upright Piano

–After James Wright

Her eyes move up to a jumble of photographs,
hockey trophies, the snow globe
they brought back from Niagara on their 25th,
the picture of two sons as toddlers, their mouths full
of question marks —
birthdays, weddings, family picnics that stretched
into the distances of the afternoon,
and later — graduations — her sons
fully grown and full of answers.

She'd always meant to pick up where the lessons
left her — learn to play the classics.
The thing that's stopping her from dusting
the keys and pulling up the black
trunk is not that it's too late to learn —
it's the nagging fear she will learn too late
she has wasted her life.

SUSAN OLDING

Making Dumplings with Chairman Mao

On Practice
Man's knowledge depends mainly on his activity in material production.

As usual, you give the orders and divide the labour. I roll the dough while you prepare the filling. You dice the cabbage, grind the pork, pound the particulars to a glutinous pulp. My wrappers, those delicate skins, you stuff and prod and pinch until they're plumper than the bourgeoisie. You range them before us like soldiers — dozens, hundreds, millions — consigning them to the boil in precise and deliberate lines.

On Contradiction
The fundamental cause of the development of a thing is not external but internal; it lies in the contradictoriness within the thing.

Didn't your mother ever show you how to seal *jiaozi*? Force will never bind them. You need to trace their edges with water — that subtle, that slippery element.

LISE ROCHEFORT

Anaïs Nin is My Analyst

First session, fair warning: *My therapy's sexperiential,*
said Nin, her 'r's', honeyed turrón, rolled on pink tongue and
palate. Flamenco's first up: My heels pound out thunder, their
click-clack staccato stilled only by — plantar fasciitis — The couch
of course, was *de rigueur*; although yes, I admit to being taken
aback when Henry and June joined us on it... Placebo effect? I
think not... Since for the first time in ages, I'm truly at peace with
Pater's passing... *Safe milieu* saw me paint each room of my
condo a different colour; creating my own little Louveciennes.
But I became so obsessed *(through transference)* with the poetry of
paint names: *ah, Italian Straw, Mink,* and *Rubidoux*, that my lie box
overflowed and I couldn't keep my stories straight, what with
lovers in Bali, So Cal and New York. Still, my functioning's
improved. And I just got my dream job: Writing erotic tales
peppered with paint-chip names, on the net! What can I say,
Anaïs? It's a marketing niche. It's a thing, it's legit... Have some
chocolate with your churros... I'll call Otto.

SUSAN WISMER

Momma's Prayer Flags

For prayer flags,
I believe I may need the Buddha
Dalai Lama, Thich Nhat Hanh—

Not being Buddhist
I don't think it's right
To call on them now in my moment of need
Although, I expect they would be kind.

Perhaps the Virgin Mary.
God,
Seeing we are unworthy
Gives His graces to her.

The truth is, I'm not Catholic either

What about Shakespeare?
I still have my mother's copy of
His collected works.

It's Brigid I come to.
I bring her my tattered prayers,
Tie rags on the hawthorn tree
At her sacred well—

May I be worthy
May I be worthy enough to write
About how
I loved to help Momma hang out the laundry

And to watch the bright colours blow dry
In the wind.

Contributors

Susan Alexander is grateful for the teaching of Lorna Crozier, th hospitality of Wintergreen Studios, for a week spent writing in th straw bale "Beach House" surrounded by supportive, inspired write for company and critique. Susan's poems have appeared or a: upcoming in *CV2*, *Grain*, *Room*, *PRISM* and *Crux*.

Laura Apol is associate professor at Michigan State University. She author of three collections of her own poems: *Falling into Grac Crossing the Ladder of Sun*, and most recently, *Requiem, Rwanda*, draw from her work with survivors of the 1994 genocide against the Tutsi.

Mary Lee Bragg lives in Ottawa. She published the novel *Shooti Angels* in 2004, and has had short fiction and poetry published literary magazines, anthologies and ezines in Canada, the US ar Cuba. Her poetry chapbook *Winter Music* won the Tree Chapboc Prize in 2013.

Maureen Bauer-McGahey is a writer living near Perth, Ontario.

Sandra Campbell writes fiction and non-fiction. A Toronto Boc Award nominee, her first novel, *Getting to Normal* was named as one *NOW* magazine's best books. As a community educator, h workshops for adults and youth focus on the dynamics of the sense memory and the imagination in the creative process.

Melanie Craig-Hansford is a retired high school teacher-librarian from high school in Kingston, Ontario. Melanie received a Bachelor of Fine Arts and a Bachelor of Education from the Nova Scotia College of Art and Design in 1985. She currently lives in Erbs Cove, New Brunswick. Melanie had been writing and making artwork most of her life. Her "Sharpie" drawing is on the cover.

Barbara E. Hunt is a poet, fiction, non-fiction and screenwriter, published in literary journals, anthologies and magazines across North America including CBC Radio One and *Homemakers Magazine*. She was selected for a Diaspora Dialogues poetry mentorship in the City of Toronto and released *The Patternmaker's Crumpled Plan* (Piquant Press) in 2011.

After too many years south of the border, **Ruth McKinney** returned to Canada to find the voice she had left behind. Happily, she found her Muse still waiting on the banks of the St. Lawrence, near Kingston, where she lives with her husband and a Torby called Fiona.

Susan Olding's *Pathologies: A Life in Essays*, was chosen by *49th Shelf* and Amazon.ca as one of 100 Canadian books to read in a lifetime. She remembers her week at Wintergreen as green and golden.

Lise Rochefort is a bilingual poet and researcher living and writing in Ottawa, Ontario, and Val-des-Monts, Québec. She is *Arc Poetry Magazine's* Associate Poetry Editor and hopes to publish her first book of poetry by next... well, soon...

Susan Wismer is a poet living in Collingwood, Ontario.

Wintergreen Studios Press is an independent literary press. It is affiliated with the not-for-profit educational retreat centre, Wintergreen Studios, and supports the work of Wintergreen Studios by publishing works related to education, the arts, and the environment.

www.wintergreenstudios.com

WINTERGREEN
STUDIOS PRESS

www.ingramcontent.com/pod-product-compliance
Lightning Source LLC
Chambersburg PA
CBHW061759040426
42447CB00011B/2386